Book Marks
A Reading Tracker

BY BOOK RIOT

ABRAMS NOTERIE, NEW YORK

Index

More index
this way!

Index

SECTION	PAGES
Read Harder Reference Pages	121–141

Why Do You Read ?

IF BOOKS ARE AN ESSENTIAL PART OF YOUR LIFE—AND WE ASSUME THEY ARE BECAUSE YOU'RE THE KIND OF PERSON WHO PICKS UP A BOOKISH BULLET JOURNAL— YOU PROBABLY HAVE A MILLION ANSWERS TO THIS QUESTION . . . AND YOU PROBABLY DON'T FEEL THAT ANY OF THEM ACTUALLY EXPLAIN WHY YOU CARE SO MUCH ABOUT READING.

Books entertain us and educate us. They comfort us and challenge us. They provide us with both company and solitude. Books give us new lenses through which we make sense of the world and new language with which we understand ourselves. Reading is fun! But it's serious. It's a hobby. But it's so much more!

At Book Riot, we believe there are as many ways to be a Book Person as there are Book People in the world, and that they're all equally valid and meaningful. Some booklovers have TBR (to-be-read) lists a mile long, while others fly by the seat of their pants. Some make a point of reading eclectically, and some prefer the familiar comforts of one favorite genre. There are readers who joyfully underline important passages and those who are horrified by the suggestion of writing in a book. And that's to say nothing of the question of crafting with books!

Whatever kind of book nerd you are, and whether you've been tracking your reading for years or are just setting out on the journey, this journal is for you. We've created places for you to list the books you read and the ones you want to read, the books you've loaned to friends (you're so generous!) and the ones you're planning to read (and will pretend to have

finished) for book club. There are pages for recording wise words and new-to-you words, logging highlights from a variety of genres, and noting characters you love and love to hate. And, of course, there's plenty of open space for you to do your own thing and explore all the ways that keeping track of your reading can enrich your reading life.

As you jump in, remember: There are no *shoulds* in the reading life. Keep track of every page you read, or don't. Set an ambitious reading goal, or don't. Take meticulous notes every day, or check in whenever you remember to. This journal is yours, and it should work for you, not the other way around. Just like there's no one right way to be a reader, there's no one right way to use this book. You do you, and if you learn something about yourself along the way? Well, that's what it's all about.

Go forth and get your read on.

Make This Journal Work for You

It's a reading tracker!

It's a bullet journal!

So . . . how exactly does this work?

A bullet journal is meant to be adapted to your needs. This is a flexible, customizable place, with one real purpose: **to help you express your love of books in every and any way possible.** If you're new to bullet journaling, here's a quick primer on how to maximize these pages.

Bullet journaling starts at the **index** (essentially a table of contents), where you keep a continuous log of all the pages in your journal as a quick reference tool. The index on pages 5–6 is partially filled out with the pages we've set up for you, but there is room to add new entries (or *collections* in bullet-speak) and to add additional page numbers to existing entries.

Throughout the first section of this book you'll find **templates** to guide you in your journaling, while the rest of the book is mostly blank. (We've provided more prompts and quotes for inspiration, but if you're good by then, don't let us get in your way).

And if something in the template isn't quite to your liking, by all means, tweak it! Add a new column here, omit something there, and keep adjusting as needed. Make changes and make them work for you. That's the bullet journal way.

If you run out of space on your reading log, or you fill up the whole dedicated quotes page, or you want to write a review for every book you read, no matter! Just turn to the **blank pages**, copy the template over, and add the page number to your index.

At the back of the book are the **Read Harder Reference Pages**—use them for inspiration. We also call out some spots throughout the journal where you might want to refer to them for ideas or clarification.

NOW, HAVE AT IT!

Literary

JANUARY

01: *Frankenstein* by Mary Shelley published, 1818

03: J. R. R. Tolkien's birthday, 1892

12: Haruki Murakami's birthday, 1949

18: Winnie the Pooh Day

28: *Pride and Prejudice* by Jane Austen published, 1813

29: "The Raven" by Edgar Allan Poe published, 1845

In her monstrous debut novel, Shelley birthed the science fiction genre

Celebrated on author A. A. Milne's birthday, 1882

FEBRUARY

01: Langston Hughes's birthday, 1902

12: Judy Blume's birthday, 1938

16: LeVar Burton's birthday, 1957

23: W. E. B. DuBois's birthday, 1868

A leader of the Harlem Renaissance, poet Hughes was also an activist, novelist & playwright

MAY

01: *Narrative of the Life of Frederick Douglass* by Frederick Douglas published, 1845

12: Limerick Day

14: *Mrs. Dalloway* by Virginia Woolf published, 1925

25: Towel Day

25: Ralph Waldo Emerson's birthday, 1803

31: Walt Whitman's birthday, 1819

Celebrated in honor of Edward Lear, best known for popularizing limericks, who was born on this day, 1812

Referring to The Hitchhiker's Guide to the Galaxy, which establishes that a towel is "about the most massively useful thing an interstellar hitchhiker can have."

JUNE

07: Nikki Giovanni's birthday, 1943

12: Anne Frank receives a diary for her birthday, 1942

16: Bloomsday

17: *Things Fall Apart* published, 1958

22: Octavia Butler's birthday, 1947

26: *Harry Potter and the Philosopher's Stone* by J. K. Rowling published in the UK, 1997

Annual celebration of author James Joyce's life and work, occurring on the day his novel Ulysses takes place in 1904

SEPTEMBER

10: Mary Oliver's birthday, 1935

15: Agatha Christie's birthday, 1890

17: Oprah's Book Club launched, 1996

18: *Their Eyes Were Watching God* by Zora Neale Hurston published, 1937

21: Stephen King's birthday, 1947

25: National Comic Book Day

Oliver won both the Pulitzer Prize and the National Book Award in a career that spanned five decades

The groundbreaking writer was the first black woman of any nationality to be awarded the prize.

OCTOBER

03: BookRiot.com launches, 2011

07: Toni Morrison wins the Nobel Prize in Literature, 1993

10: *The New York Times* publishes its first book review section, 1896

21: Ursula K. LeGuin's birthday, 1929

31: First collection of *The Adventures of Sherlock Holmes* by Sir Arthur Conan Doyle published, 1892

It ran a piece on Oscar Wilde and news about a group of independent booksellers working to combat competition from department stores

Holidays

MARCH

02: Read Across America Day

04: National Grammar Day

10: The first Book of the Month selection is published, 1926

21: World Poetry Day

26: Robert Frost's Birthday, 1874

Annual celebration of children's literacy, observed on Dr. Seuss's birthday, 1904

Also the anniversary of Shakespeare's death, 1616

APRIL

The first living writer to have her work published by the Library of America

04: Maya Angelou's birthday, 1928

10: *The Great Gatsby* published, 1925

13: Eudora Welty's birthday, 1909

14: First edition of *Webster's American Dictionary of the English Language* published, 1828

23: World Book Day

24: The Library of Congress is created, 1800

JULY

10: Alice Munro's birthday, 1931

11: *To Kill a Mockingbird* by Harper Lee published, 1960

18: Nelson Mandela's birthday, 1918

30: Paperback books first introduced in the US by Penguin books, 1935

31: Harry Potter's birthday, 1980

The novel was originally published as a weekly serial

The Boy Who Lived shares a birthday with his creator, J. K. Rowling

But German publisher Albatross Books first experimented with the format in 1931

AUGUST

02: James Baldwin's birthday, 1924

03: The final installment of *Great Expectations* by Charles Dickens published, 1861

09: National Book Lovers Day

22: Dorothy Parker's birthday, 1893

22: Ray Bradbury's birthday, 1920

Fun fact: Many of Dickinson's poems can be sung to the tune of the Gilligan's Island theme song.

NOVEMBER

01: National Family Literacy Day

08: Margaret Mitchell's birthday, 1900

18: *Calvin and Hobbes* by Bill Watterson first published, 1985

28: Truman Capote throws landmark Black and White Ball, 1966

29: Madeleine L'Engle's birthday, 1918

He selected Katharine Graham, publisher of the Washington Post, as the guest of honor

DECEMBER

05: Joan Didion's birthday, 1934

10: Emily Dickinson's birthday, 1830

14: Shirley Jackson's birthday, 1916

24: Jolabokaflod celebrated

The Icelandic tradition of exchanging books on Christmas Eve and spending the evening reading them

Templates

THE FOLLOWING PAGES CONTAIN SOME OF OUR FAVORITE
WAYS TO SET UP AND USE YOUR JOURNAL. START BY FILLING
THEM OUT, AND WHEN YOU'RE DONE, COPY THE TEMPLATE
OVER TO THE BLANK PAGES AND KEEP IT GOING.

These collections are already noted in your index. There are pages
for tracking the total number of books you read, writing reviews,
illustrating your favorite reads, and even playing a Read Harder–inspired
book bingo board. Use these templates as a jumping-off point for your
book-tracking journey.

READ ON!

Author Stats

e.g., American, British, etc.

Who are you reading?

Tick these as you read.

NATIONALITY							GENDER		
							M	F	NB

AGE RANGE													
under 30													
30–39													
40–49													
50+													

Book Facts

What are you reading?

YEAR OF PUBLICATION										
PRE 1900S										
1900-1949										
1950-1999										
2000-PRESENT										

See pages 121–141 for some genre examples.

GENRE								

Reading Log

TITLE / AUTHOR	FINISHED

TITLE / AUTHOR	FINISHED

We know you'll fill these pages up quickly, so we added a second reading log on the next pages.

Reading Log

TITLE / AUTHOR	FINISHED

TITLE / AUTHOR	FINISHED

Out of room again? Continue your log on the blank pages that start on page 45.

Book Reviews

Reviews come in all shapes and sizes. Have some fun playing around with types of reviews to find the style that suits you.

THREE-WORD REVIEWS

Keep it simple: Describe this book in three words.

TITLE: _____ AUTHOR: _____

TITLE: _____ AUTHOR: _____

TITLE: _____ AUTHOR: _____

ONE-SENTENCE REVIEWS

TITLE: _____ AUTHOR: _____

TITLE: _____ AUTHOR: _____

TITLE: _____ AUTHOR: _____

Getting longer: Try reviewing
the book in just a sentence.

Book Reviews

FYI—these are short recommendations posted under a book in stores, written by staff. Try to really sell someone on the book!

SHELF TALKERS

Illustrate the cover!

TITLE: _____ AUTHOR: _____

REVIEW:

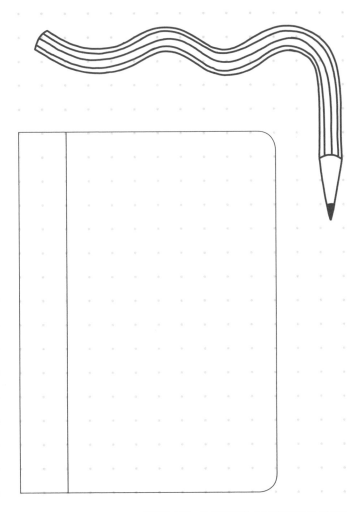

TITLE: _____ AUTHOR: _____

REVIEW:

Book Reviews

LONG-FORM REVIEW
TITLE:
AUTHOR:
PUBLISHER/IMPRINT:
PUBLICATION DATE:
FORMAT: HARDCOVER, PAPERBACK, E-BOOK, AUDIO
DISCOVERY:
DATE STARTED: **DATE FINISHED:**
REVIEW: RATING ☆ ☆ ☆ ☆ ☆
NOTES & QUOTES:

How did you find out
about this book?

Take note of other
details in this
extended review

LONG-FORM REVIEW

TITLE:

AUTHOR:

PUBLISHER/IMPRINT:

PUBLICATION DATE:

FORMAT: HARDCOVER, PAPERBACK, E-BOOK, AUDIO

DISCOVERY:

DATE STARTED: **DATE FINISHED:**

REVIEW: **RATING** ☆ ☆ ☆ ☆ ☆

NOTES & QUOTES:

BOOK BINGO

Challenge yourself to read different types of books through a game of bingo—Read Harder edition! Check out page 121 for more on the Read Harder challenge. Bonus points for a blackout.

A RETELLING OF A CLASSIC STORY	A BOOK PUBLISHED BY AN INDIE PUBLISHER OR MICROPRESS
AN AUDIE AWARD-WINNING AUDIOBOOK	A NOVEL BY A TRANS OR NONBINARY AUTHOR
A BOOK ABOUT TECHNOLOGY	A BOOK THAT WON THE NATIONAL BOOK AWARD, MAN BOOKER PRIZE, OR PULITZER PRIZE IN THE LAST YEAR
A BOOK WRITTEN BY SOMEONE WHEN THEY WERE OVER THE AGE OF 65	A BOOK PUBLISHED BEFORE 1900
A SELF-PUBLISHED BOOK	A BOOK ABOUT NATURE

A BOOK THAT HAS BEEN BANNED OR FREQUENTLY CHALLENGED IN YOUR COUNTRY	A BOOK WITH A COVER YOU HATE	A BOOK WRITTEN BY SOMEONE WHEN THEY WERE UNDER THE AGE OF 25
A NEW PLAY PUBLISHED IN THE LAST YEAR	A BOOK IN WHICH AN ANIMAL OR INANIMATE OBJECT IS A POINT-OF-VIEW CHARACTER	AN ASSIGNED BOOK YOU HATED OR NEVER FINISHED BEFORE NOW
Book of Your Choice	A BOOK PUBLISHED POSTHUMOUSLY	A CLASSIC BY AN AUTHOR OF COLOR
A BOOK WRITTEN BY AN IMMIGRANT	A BOOK ABOUT BOOKS	A BOOK RECOMMENDED BY A FRIEND
A BOOK MORE THAN 500 PAGES LONG	A BOOK TRANSLATED BY A WOMAN	A CHILDREN'S BOOK OR YA NOVEL PUBLISHED IN THE LAST YEAR

Favorites Shelf

Fill these shelves
with your all-time
favorite reads!

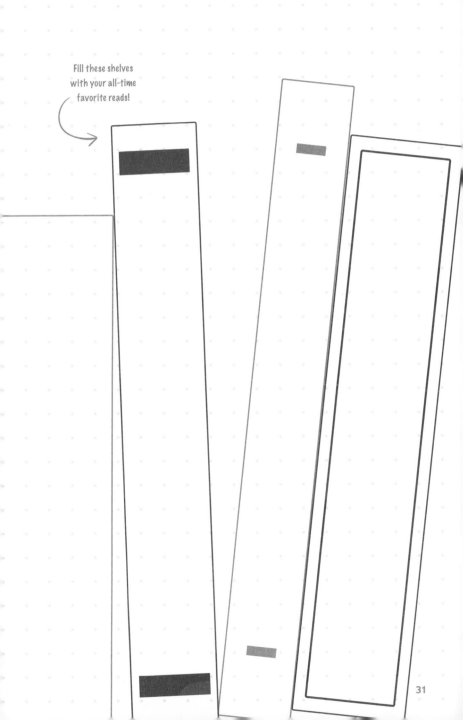

Found Text-Book

Text comes at you every minute of your life: through books, yes, but also in headlines, tweets, texts, quotes, signs, graffiti, song lyrics, overheard conversations, and more. Challenge yourself to log one tidbit of text you encounter—from a few words to a sentence—every day for a month to create a unique diary of found words. Who knows what inspiration will arise?

MONTH: _____

1.

2.

3.

4.

5.

6.

7.

8.

9.

10.

11.

12.

13.

14.

15.

16.

17.

18.

19.

20.

21.

22.

23.

24.

25.

26.

27.

28.

29.

30.

31.

Favorite Quotes

Letter the wittiest, most poetic, or just downright inspiring quotes that you come across or jot down some of your favorite passages.

Word Bank

Keep a running list of all-new words picked up in your reading.

WORD	PICKED UP FROM	DEFINITION

Lending Library

Never lose track of a book again!

TITLE	LOANED TO/BORROWED FROM

Characters of Note

Take a cue from yearbook superlatives and write the names of or draw the characters you encounter in your reading.

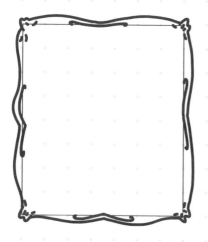

BEST CHARACTER ARC

DREAMIEST

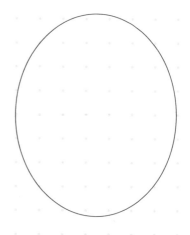

MOST QUESTIONABLE MOTIVES

BEST VILLAIN

How to Find a Book Club

WHETHER YOU'RE LOOKING TO MEET LIKE-MINDED READERS, ENGAGE WITH YOUR COMMUNITY, OR JUST HAVE ANOTHER EXCUSE TO HANG OUT WITH FRIENDS, BEING PART OF A BOOK CLUB CAN TURN THE NORMALLY SOLITARY ACT OF READING INTO A SOCIAL ACTIVITY. HERE ARE SOME WAYS TO FIND THE ONE THAT'S RIGHT FOR YOU.

Bookstores: Many independent bookstores hold book clubs as a way to reach and engage with the bookish community. Head to your favorite indie in person or on social media for club updates.

Libraries: Already have a library card? It's likely your local branch hosts a book club or two. Not only are they led by top-notch staff, but the library will usually have copies of the book on hand.

Online: There are plenty of opportunities to talk books online: Goodreads provides an old-school forum, while Twitter, Facebook, and Instagram are modern chat resources (that may require a bit more digging to find what you're looking for). And of course, we're talking books all day, every day at Book Riot!

Celebrity Clubs: There's also a whole world of celebrity book clubs to partake in, from Oprah's Book Club to Our Shared Shelf, an intersectional feminist book club founded by Emma Watson, to Reese Witherspoon's women-centric club. Look for stickers on books proclaiming the selection, or follow celebs on social media for the most reliable updates.

Where else?: Beyond bookstores, other brick and mortars like bars, cafés, and even specialty shops like craft stores sometimes host book club meet ups. Ask around and scope out spots in your neighborhood. Who knows what secret gatherings and fellow book nerds you may encounter!

Discussion Notes

Fill out this page for your next book club discussion.

TITLE:
AUTHOR:
FAVORITE PASSAGES:
SOURCES OF CONFUSION:
OTHER THOUGHTS:

Re-create this template for
future book club notes.

How to Start Your Own Club

NOT FINDING THE CLUB THAT'S RIGHT FOR YOU? SOMETIMES YOU JUST HAVE TO DO IT YOURSELF. HERE'S HOW TO GET A BOOK CLUB OF YOUR OWN OFF THE GROUND.

Choose a theme: What sort of books do you want to read? All bestsellers? Nonfiction titles? Do you want to start a cookbook club? Or a classics club? Having a theme makes the book selection process easier and unites the members, but if you don't want to limit yourself to a specific type of read, we're not going to stop you.

Gather your group: Figure out who's joining you in this venture. Are you meeting with a close group of friends who you already swap books with? Do you want to establish a club at your workplace? Are you trying to meet new people? Think about the purpose of your book club—is it to read? Primarily to socialize? Both?

Lock it down: Next, pick a spot and time to meet. It could be in people's homes, in a public space, or even online through social media or on a dedicated site. Most groups meet monthly at a regular time for scheduling efficiency. Communicate to all your members when the club will meet and keep an organized schedule.

Pick the book: You have your group, your theme, your meeting place—now, what exactly to read? Even though as founder you may be the de facto club leader, selecting the book that everyone will be reading is best left to democracy. If conversation doesn't naturally flow to the next selection, sending out an online poll makes the process quick and anonymous.

Final notes: Before your club meets, think about how you want the session to be run. Are you going to lead the group in discussion? Plan out activities? Will there be snacks? Clearly lay out expectations before everyone gathers—if the purpose is really to talk about the book, people should come prepared. But be attuned to the group and see how the meeting evolves.

Blank Pages

DEAR READER: YOU HAVE THE TOOLS, YOU HAVE THE BOOKS, YOU HAVE YOUR WITS – YOU'RE ON YOUR OWN NOW. AHEAD, EMPTY PAGES AWAIT YOU, ALONG WITH THE FREEDOM TO EXPAND ON ANY COLLECTION YOU'VE COMPLETED OR TO START A BRAND-NEW ONE.

If you're looking for inspiration, there are list prompts and quotes sprinkled throughout, and at the end of the book are Read Harder reference pages with suggestions for your next book. Maybe after all this reading you will have a spark of an idea for a story of your own, in which case, why not hammer it out here? Or maybe you want to use every one of these pages for logging specific book entries, and that's cool too. Whatever happens next is up to you.

Favorite first lines:

> "Reading brings us unknown friends."

HONORÉ DE BALZAC

Unsettling endings:

"If a book is well written, I always find it too short."

JANE AUSTEN

Books I want to reread:

> **"Through it [literature] we know the past, govern the present, and influence the future."**
>
> CHARLOTTE PERKINS GILMAN

Books that changed my point of view:

"To learn to read is to light a fire; every syllable spelled out is a spark."

VICTOR HUGO

Favorite childhood reads:

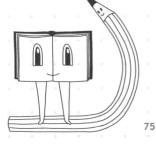

"Books are the mirrors of the soul."

VIRGINIA WOOLF

Books I just couldn't finish:

"'Tis the good reader that makes the good book."

RALPH WALDO EMERSON

Favorite authors:

> "A book must be the axe for the frozen sea within us."

FRANZ KAFKA

Books I can't stop thinking about:

"Reading is my favorite occupation."

ANNE BRONTË

Favorite flawed characters:

> "It is what
> you read
> when you
> don't have
> to that
> determines
> what you
> will be when
> you can't
> help it."

CHARLES FRANCIS POTTER

Favorite bookstores:

"I like to
eat, sleep,
drink, and
be in love.
I like to
work, read,
learn, and
understand
life."

LANGSTON HUGHES

Read Harder Reference Pages

IT IS A TRUTH UNIVERSALLY ACKNOWLEDGED, HERE AT BOOK RIOT, THAT THERE IS NO RIGHT WAY TO READ, JUST AS THERE IS NO RIGHT TYPE OF BOOK. WHETHER YOU'RE READING TO LEARN AND GROW AS A READER OR AS A MEANS OF ESCAPE OR AMUSEMENT, WHAT MATTERS IS THAT YOU ARE READING. PERIOD.

We started the Read Harder Challenge in 2015 to promote reading diversity at every level. Each year we release a list of twenty-four reading prompts to help readers expand their reading habits and seek out new books that they may not have found on their own. Read Harder emphasizes variety, not quantity: By reading more broadly, you'll discover the magic of words in new ways, through authors with fresh perspectives from places near, far, and imagined, and from cultures different than your own.

Now we're broadening the scope of Read Harder by taking a look at some of the major publishing categories and giving you an in. Curious about reading YA as an adult? Never given genre fiction a try? Eager for a digestible cookbook? Let us break them down for you . . .

Young Adult

YOUNG ADULT BOOKS SPAN ALL GENRES AND OFFER UP STORIES TOLD FROM THE PERSPECTIVES OF TEEN-AGERS NAVIGATING THE WORLD THE BEST THEY CAN. AND THEY'RE NOT JUST FOR TEEN READERS! THE ISSUES YOUNG PEOPLE FACE ARE UNIVERSAL, AND THEIR STO-RIES ARE COMPELLING WHETHER YOU'RE IN THE MIDST OF YOUR OWN TEENAGE EXPERIENCE OR LOOKING AT IT IN THE REARVIEW MIRROR.

READ HARDER!

- **Read a YA or middle-grade novel by an author who identifies as LGBTQIA+**

- **Read a translated YA novel**

- **Read the first book in a new-to-you YA or middle-grade series**

- **Read a YA book in one sitting**

- **Read a genre-bending YA book**

NICE TO MEET YA

BOOK RIOT SUGGESTS:

We Set the Dark on Fire **by Tehlor Kay Mejia:** Compelling, immersive, and beautifully written, this feminist read is for anyone who enjoys mythology, stories of taking down power, and the dynamics of female relationships as they exist in a world meant to keep girls as enemies, rather than as friends or lovers.

Here to Stay **by Sara Farizan:** Bijan's winning shot during a high-stakes basketball game brings him glory and newfound popularity, but also Islamophobic cyberbullying in this poignant, sports-driven, and funny (really!) contemporary read.

Blood Water Paint **by Joy McCullough:** Told in verse, this historical novel fictionalizes the real-life story of Italian artist Artemisia Gentileschi, whose mother died when she was twelve, leaving her with a choice that would shape the rest of her life: become a nun, or spend her days grinding pigment for her father's paint.

Dry **by Neal & Jarrod Shusterman:** Water runs dry in Southern California, and things turn desperate and feral in this all-too-possible novel about climate change.

Our Stories, Our Voices: 21 YA Authors Get Real About Injustice, Empowerment, and Growing Up Female in America **edited by Amy Reed:** Twenty-one female-identifying writers share essays about what it means to strive for justice, what it means to be empowered, how much work has been done in the last few decades, and how much work is left to be done for equality and beyond.

Self Help

ONE OF THE BEST WAYS TO BETTER YOURSELF, ACQUIRE NEW SKILLS, OR SIMPLY UNDERSTAND HOW YOU AND OTHER HUMANS OPERATE, IS THROUGH A GOOD SELF-HELP/SELF-DEVELOPMENT BOOK. UP YOUR CREATIVITY, SHARPEN YOUR LEADERSHIPS SKILLS, FIND JOY IN THE EVERYDAY, AND MORE.

READ HARDER!

- **Read a business book**
- **Read a book on social science**
- **Read a motivational book**
- **Read a fitness or health book**
- **Read a non-traditional self-help book (something on creativity or spirituality, or a guided journal)**

BOOK RIOT SUGGESTS:

***Brave, Not Perfect: Fear Less, Fail More, and Live Bolder* by Reshma Saujani:** Throw out the idea that to be brave, you need to be perfect. This book is about embracing imperfection, finding courage, and taking risks.

***Dare to Lead: Brave Work. Tough Conversations. Whole Hearts.* by Brené Brown:** Learn how to be a leader, both in your workplace and in your own life, by understanding and incorporating empathy into every interaction. A great introduction to some of the biggest ideas Brown has set forth.

***Bored and Brilliant: How Spacing Out Can Unlock Your Most Productive and Creative Self* by Manoush Zomorodi:** No need to toss out your technology to up your focus, your concentration, and your creativity. Instead, Zomorodi offers practical steps for incorporating more boredom into your life, which will allow those things to arise more naturally.

***Creative Quest* by Questlove:** Life lessons and applicable ideas from well-known cultural omnivore Questlove, who shares his own stories and suggests ways you too can build more fun and creativity into your everyday life. This one's especially excellent on audiobook.

***Joyful: The Surprising Power of Ordinary Things to Create Extraordinary Happiness* by Ingrid Fetell Lee:** Lee's uplifting and energetic book encourages everyone to actively make room for more joy in the everyday, whether at home, the office, or anywhere else.

Mystery, Thriller & Suspense

WHETHER YOU'RE IN IT FOR THE THRILL OF THE CHASE OR THE SATISFACTION OF THE SOLVE, HERE ARE FIVE CRIME BOOKS SURE TO FILL THE WIDE RANGE OF MYSTERY AND THRILLER-LOVING HEARTS OUT THERE—OR TO MAKE A MYSTERY FAN OUT OF YOU!

READ HARDER!

- Read a book of true crime
- Read a translated novel
- Read a cozy mystery
- Read a book that was adapted into a movie (then watch the movie!)
- Read a horror book

BOOK RIOT SUGGESTS:

The Rachel Getty and Esa Khattak **series by Ausma Zehanat Khan:** A smart, thoughtful, and intense series that travels the world while following Canadian detectives who work on minority-sensitive cases—perfect for procedural fans!

Death Notice **by Zhou Haohui, translated by Zac Haluza:** A great cat-and-mouse thriller about a vigilante, Eumenides, who toys with the police as he exacts revenge on those he feels deserve to be punished ...

The Widows of Malabar Hill **by Sujata Massey:** This delightful historical mystery follows Perveen Mistry, the first female lawyer in Bombay, who has a moral compass that points to helping others at all costs.

Death Prefers Blondes **by Caleb Roehrig:** Imagine if *Ocean's 11* dated *RuPaul's Drag Race* and the wedding reception got crashed by *Hamlet*—that's this awesome heist thriller led by a teen girl and her crew of drag queens.

The Red Parts **by Maggie Nelson:** A true-crime memoir—and meditation on humanity and society—written by the niece of Jane Mixer, whose 1969 murder went unsolved until 2004.

Nonfiction

IT'S ALMOST NOT FAIR TO PUT ALL NONFICTION TOGETHER BECAUSE THERE ARE SO MANY SUBJECTS, SUBCATEGORIES, APPROACHES, AND STYLES TO EXPLORE. BUT THAT'S PART OF THE FUN. WHETHER YOU'RE A STRICTLY-FICTION READER LOOKING TO BRANCH OUT OR A LONGTIME NONFIC FAN, WE THINK YOU'LL FIND SOMETHING TO BROADEN YOUR HORIZONS IN THE BOOKS BELOW.

READ HARDER!

- **Read an essay anthology**
- **Read a book about sports**
- **Read a book on hard science**
- **Read a humor nonfiction book**
- **Read a book about art history**

BOOK RIOT SUGGESTS:

The Boys in the Boat: Nine Americans and Their Epic Quest for Gold at the 1936 Berlin Olympics **by Daniel James Brown:** You'll be at the edge of your seat reading this page-turning history of nine working-class college students from Washington and their quest to defeat the elite crew teams of the East Coast for a chance to row for gold in the Olympics.

The Warmth of Other Suns: The Epic Story of America's Great Migration **by Isabel Wilkerson:** Through the stories of three people, this book shares the broad impact of the mass migration of black citizens from the South to cities in the North and the West seeking safety and economic opportunity in the mid-twentieth century.

The Emperor of All Maladies: A Biography of Cancer **by Siddhartha Mukherjee:** Don't let the length of this one deter you—this history of cancer is a readable, empathetic, and deeply researched look at how humans have battled against a disease for more than five thousand years.

The Empathy Exams **by Leslie Jamison:** This collection of essays ties together stories of medical acting, poverty tourism, street violence, and reality television to explore how we care about each other and understand other people's pain.

The Dragon Behind the Glass: A True Story of Power, Obsession, and the World's Most Coveted Fish **by Emily Voigt:** In this book, a journalist sets out to find the world's most expensive aquarium fish, the Asian arowana, in the wild, sparking a globe-spanning adventure that leads to stories of murder, pet detectives, and modern science.

Biography & Memoir

PEOPLE ARE INTERESTING, AND EVERY LIFE CONTAINS IMPORTANT STORIES THAT ARE WORTHY OF SHARING, WHETHER THEY'RE A CELEBRITY OR AN AVERAGE JANE. SOME WRITERS TELL THEIR OWN STORIES, SOME TELL OTHERS' STORIES, AND SOME, WELL, TAKE A LITTLE CREATIVE LICENSE (MEMOIR, WE'RE LOOKING AT YOU). BIOGRAPHIES: THEY'RE NOT JUST FOR FATHER'S DAY ANYMORE!

READ HARDER!

- **Read an illustrated memoir**
- **Read a travel memoir**
- **Read a biography of someone completely unknown to you**
- **Read a coming-of-age memoir**
- **Read an autobiography**

BOOK RIOT SUGGESTS:

The Good Neighbor: The Life and Work of Fred Rogers **by Maxwell King:** Fred Rogers was the inspiring host of a show beloved by several generations of children. And there was so much more to his life and work than most viewers knew! Learn the whole story, and get your tissues ready—it's a good one.

Heavy: An American Memoir **by Kiese Laymon:** The word *unflinching* gets thrown around a lot when talking memoirs, but this one actually fits the bill. Laymon shines a bright light on issues related to race, body image, and deep family trauma, and man, does he know how to write a sentence.

When Women Were Birds: Fifty-Four Variations on Voice **by Terry Tempest Williams:** When her mother died, Terry Tempest Williams inherited her journals. And they were all blank. Why had her mother intentionally kept a shelf full of blank journals? What does it mean to have a voice? This one-of-a-kind memoir seeks to explore these questions, and many more.

Girl Sleuth: Nancy Drew and the Women Who Created Her **by Melanie Rehak:** Did you know that Carolyn Keene wasn't the author of the Nancy Drew series, but a pseudonym for the group of writers who created it? Neither did we! Get the inside scoop on one of literature's most beloved kid detectives in this fascinating biography.

Is Everyone Hanging Out Without Me? (And Other Concerns) **by Mindy Kaling:** If you're skeptical of celebrity memoirs or suspicious that they're more style than substance, let Mindy Kaling prove you wrong as she writes about childhood, ambition, Hollywood, friendship, dating woes, and more. Pro tip: listen to this one on audio. It's like hanging out with a smart, hilarious friend.

Sci-Fi & Fantasy

SCIENCE FICTION, FANTASY, AND SPECULATIVE FICTION ENCOMPASS A MULTITUDE OF SUBGENRES THAT REMOVE READERS FROM THE KNOWN AND TRANSPORT THEM INTO FAIRYTALE WORLDS, MYTHOLOGIES, DEEP SPACE, ALTERNATE HISTORIES, THE FUTURE, AND ANY TIME AND PLACE BEYOND THE REALM OF REALITY THAT ONE MIGHT IMAGINE.

READ HARDER!

- **Read an alternate history novel**
- **Read a book based on mythology or folklore**
- **Read a dystopian or post-apocalyptic novel**
- **Read a novel by an author of color**
- **Read a novel with a female protagonist by a female author**

BOOK RIOT SUGGESTS:

Black Leopard, Red Wolf by **Marlon James:** Incorporating African mythology and history, this epic fantasy is perfect for readers looking to jump into the deep end of the genre with an immersive and visceral quest featuring stellar worldbuilding.

Moon of the Crusted Snow by **Waubgeshig Rice:** Following a northern Anishinaabe community cut off from electricity, this apocalyptic First Nation story packs power and intensity into a short, fast-paced read, ideal for new and veteran sci-fi readers alike.

The Long Way to a Small, Angry Planet by **Becky Chambers:** If you think science fiction can't be fun, this space opera, which follows a ragtag crew risking it all aboard the spaceship equivalent of a jalopy, is here to disprove you. (Be prepared to tear through the addictive adventure series!)

What Is Not Yours Is Not Yours by **Helen Oyeyemi:** Fans of short stories and readers seeking the uncanny will want to check out this collection built around the theme of keys. Enjoy a compelling introduction to one of the best contemporary writers of magical realism.

The City in the Middle of the Night by **Charlie Jane Anders:** Go on an unforgettable odyssey across a planet divided between frozen darkness and endless sunshine, and gather a motley family along the way—you're in safe hands on your sci-fi journey with this Hugo Award–winning author and former editor in chief of popular SFF site io9.

Cooking

COOKING CAN BE INTIMIDATING! THERE ARE ALL KINDS OF TECHNIQUES AND UNFAMILIAR TERMINOLOGY, AND YOU MIGHT NEED NEW TOOLS. FEAR NOT! THESE GREAT BOOKS WILL GIVE YOU THE BASICS AND THEN SOME. ALONG THE WAY, YOU MAY DISCOVER THE PLEASURE OF READING THE STORIES AND RECIPES OR METHODS, EVEN WITHOUT ATTEMPTING THEM.

READ HARDER!

- **Read a James Beard Award–winning cookbook**
- **Read a cookbook you have never thought to try**
- **Read a cookbook published in the twentieth century**
- **Read a regional cookbook from the last place you traveled to**
- **Read a technique-specific cookbook**

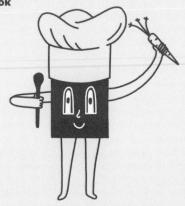

BOOK RIOT SUGGESTS:

Salt, Fat, Acid, Heat: Mastering the Elements of Good Cooking **by Samin Nosrat:** True to the promise of its title, this comprehensive cookbook explains the foundational ingredients of cooking. In charming, accessible prose, Nosrat provides instruction on fundamental kitchen techniques and includes a ton of delicious recipes, all with whimsical illustrations. Perfect for novices and experienced cooks alike.

Appetites: A Cookbook **by Anthony Bourdain:** The late, great Bourdain broke out as a bad-boy chef memoirist and ultimately became an advocate for the power of travel and what food can teach us about cultures. Here, he celebrates the food he loved when he was off the clock, cooking for friends and family.

Buttermilk Graffiti: A Chef's Journey to Discover America's New Melting-Pot Cuisine **by Edward Lee:** The food memoir is far from new, but Lee's take is wholly original. The acclaimed chef and writer (if there's any heir to Bourdain's throne, it's him) spends two years traveling across America to understand the deep ties between culture and cooking and what our food says about who we are.

Dining In: Highly Cookable Recipes **by Alison Roman:** It's a real magic trick to elevate food without resorting to lofty language and highbrow, hard-to-find ingredients, and Roman pulls it off beautifully. The recipes in this book are simple but far from boring, and they work for everything from simple weeknight meals to impress-your-friends dinner parties.

Sister Pie: The Recipes and Stories of a Big-Hearted Bakery in Detroit **by Lisa Ludwinski:** Crack the code to perfect pie crust, get creative with flavor combinations, and even it all out with delicious salad recipes (yes, salads in a bakery book!) from the founder of a bakery that aims to change the world through food.

Comics & Graphic Novel

TALK ABOUT A MISUNDERSTOOD CATEGORY OF BOOKS! IN THE SIMPLEST TERMS, COMICS USE IMAGES AND TEXT TO TELL A STORY. THERE ARE PROBABLY AS MANY WAYS TO TELL A STORY THROUGH COMICS AS THERE ARE STORIES TO TELL, SO WE'VE FEATURED FIVE OF THE MOST COMMON APPROACHES IN THE LIST BELOW, EACH WITH A RECOMMENDATION TO HELP YOU DIVE IN.

READ HARDER!

- **Read an all-ages comic**
- **Read a manga book**
- **Read a comic with a female lead**
- **Read a comic written and illustrated by the same person**
- **Read a non-superhero comic that debuted in the last five years**

A GRAPHIC MEMOIR is an illustrated, sequential telling of the story of a person's life, in their own words. *Book Riot suggests:* **March, Books 1–3 by John Lewis, Andrew Aydin, Nate Powell (artist):** Congressman and civil rights icon John Lewis tells the story of his life, from his birth to sharecroppers in Alabama to his role in the American civil rights movement and beyond.

ALL-AGES COMICS are exactly what they sound like: comics for all readers, from young kids up! *Book Riot suggests:* **Lumberjanes, Vol 1: Beware the Kitten Holy by Noelle Stevenson, Grace Ellis, Shannon Watters, Brooke A. Allen (illustrator):** A scrappy and diverse group of friends at Miss Qiunzilla Thiskwin Penniquiqul Thistle Crumpet's summer camp for hard-core lady-types discover that they are probably in danger from several magical beasties, and use their der-ring-do to save the day!

MYSTERY COMICS: crime-solving, natch. *Book Riot suggests:* **My Favorite Thing is Monsters by Emil Ferris:** Set in 1960s Chicago (an excellent backdrop for some noir feelings if there ever was one), this is the story of ten-year-old Karen Reyes, who sets out to solve the murder of her upstairs neighbor, a Holocaust survivor named Anka, who had suspicious connections to Karen's own brother.

A SPACE OPERA is a melodramatic story of adventure, romance, and risk, set in space. Sounds rad, right? *Book Riot suggests:* **Saga by Brian K. Vaughan and Fiona Staples (artist):** The epic—and ongoing—tale of two people from worlds that are at war with each other who fall in love and have a baby . . . a baby both governments will stop at nothing to destroy. See, we told you there'd be melodrama.

FANTASY COMICS are comics about myths, magic, spells, and other other-worldly things. You know fantasy books? It's like those, but told with images too. *Book Riot suggests:* **Monstress by Marjorie M. Liu, Sana Takeda (artist)** A beautiful and brutal comic about a teenage warrior in an alternate-universe matriarchal Asia (sort of, plus magic and witches and beasts, oh my), who must solve the mystery of her connection to an ancient god in order to save herself and her world.

Poetry

AH, POETRY, THE MOST MISUNDERSTOOD OF GENRES. MAYBE YOU THINK YOU "JUST CAN'T GET INTO POETRY," OR MAYBE YOU'RE SCARRED FROM SCHOOL AND THINK ALL POETRY IS COMPLICATED AND HARD TO UNDERSTAND. POUND FOR POUND, WORD FOR WORD, POETRY PACKS A MORE POWERFUL PUNCH THAN ANY OTHER FORMAT OF WRITING. HERE ARE SOME AMAZING COLLECTIONS TO HELP YOU FIND YOUR WAY IN.

READ HARDER!

- **Read a poetry collection published before you were born**
- **Read a poetry collection by an author of color**
- **Read a translated collection of poetry**
- **Read an epic poem**
- **Read a collection of poetry by your current poet laureate**

BOOK RIOT SUGGESTS:

***New and Selected Poems, Volume One* by Mary Oliver:** Oliver believed poetry should be accessible and relatable, and her approach worked: She won numerous awards and is one of the best-selling poets in American history. These poems celebrate nature, humanity, and our connection to the natural world, and you'll probably discover that you've heard a few of them before.

***The Hungry Ear: Poems of Food and Drink* edited by Kevin Young:** Anthologies are a wonderful way to discover a bunch of new writers at once. They're low risk—you're not committed to a whole book of one person's work—and potentially high reward. This one brings together poems about food and drinking, cooking and eating, and the significance and sensuality of something we take for granted in daily life.

***Today Means Amen: Poems* by Sierra deMulder:** The title poem of this intense and intensely powerful collection went viral—deMulder is an incredible spoken-word performer and is definitely worth a Google—for very good reason. These are poems about pain and healing, fear and fierceness, love, lust, and lost.

***The Crown Ain't Worth Much* by Hanif Willis-Abdurraqib:** The poems in this collection are accessible in their format and challenging in their content. Abdurraquib writes about race, gender, family, and love through a lens that incorporates pop culture and his singular perspective.

***The Carrying* by Ada Limón:** Visceral language and vulnerable emotion make this collection of poems about the imperfect and challenging transitions of life unforgettable. Limon wrestles with aging, grief, love, joy, and the full spectrum of human emotion.

Romance

ROMANCE IS OFTEN MISREPRESENTED AS OLD-FASHIONED, SEXIST, AND POORLY WRITTEN. THESE GATEWAY ROMANCES FROM ACROSS VARIOUS SUBCATEGORIES ARE PROOF THAT IT'S ANYTHING BUT. GET READY TO GIGGLE, SWOON, AND BE SWEPT AWAY BY SMART, SELF-DETERMINED CHARACTERS AND THE DREAMY PARAMOURS WHO WIN THEIR HEARTS.

READ HARDER!

- **Read a romance by #1 bestselling author**
- **Read a romance chosen because of the title or cover**
- **Read a romance translated from another language**
- **Read a romance by an author of color**
- **Read a romance that has been adapted into a film**

BOOK RIOT SUGGESTS:

***The Duchess War* (The Brothers Sinister #1) by Courtney Milan:** Regencies—romances set in during the early nineteenth-century British regency—are a staple of romance, and Milan's spin on a wallflower with a secret past who meets a duke with secrets of his own is fun, feminist, and the start of an incredible series.

***An Extraordinary Union* (The Loyal League #1) by Alyssa Cole:** Set during the American Civil War and following a heroine and hero sent to spy on the Confederacy, this critically-acclaimed historical romance novel explores both romance and race, and is an absolute page-turner.

***Silver Silence* (Psy-Changeling Trinity #1) by Nalini Singh:** Nalini Singh is a giant in paranormal romance, and this trilogy is the perfect introduction to her fascinating world of shapeshifters and telepaths, with characters who are impossible not to root for.

***The Wedding Date* by Jasmine Guillory:** Guillory may be a relative newcomer to Romancelandia, but this take on the "fake girlfriend" rom-com trope featuring two competent, career-driven characters is a delight from start to finish.

***For Real* by Alexis Hall:** If you'd like your romance five-alarm hot (not to mention queer), Alexis Hall's contemporary erotic tale of a young dom and an older, jaded sub will turn your ears red and give you a heartache of the best kind.

Editor: Madeline Jaffe
Designer: Diane Shaw
Production Manager: Rebecca Westall

ISBN: 978-1-4197-4357-3
Text and cover © 2020 Abrams
Illustrations © 2020 Stefan Mosebach
Book Riot ® and Read Harder ® are registered trademarks of Riot New Media Group, Inc.
and are used under permission of Riot New Media Group, Inc. All rights reserved.

Printed and bound in China
10 9 8 7 6 5 4 3 2 1

Abrams Noterie products are available at special discounts when purchased in quantity
for premiums and promotions as well as fundraising or educational use. Special editions
can also be created to specification. For details, contact specialsales@abramsbooks.com
or the address below.

Abrams Noterie® is a registered trademark of Harry N. Abrams, Inc.

ABRAMS The Art of Books
195 Broadway, New York, NY 10007
abramsbooks.com

MIX
Paper from
responsible sources
FSC™ C144853